the 20th Century

The Rock Era

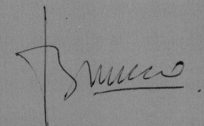

ISBN 0-634-02199-0

7777 W. BLUEMOUND RD. P.O. BOX 13819 MILWAUKEE, WI 53213

Visit Hal Leonard Online at
www.halleonard.com

CONTENTS

4 ABC
The Jackson 5

8 Angel
Sarah McLachlan

14 Another Day in Paradise
Phil Collins

18 At the Hop
Danny & The Juniors

24 Baby Love
The Supremes

26 Bohemian Rhapsody
Queen

21 Crying
Roy Orbison

36 Dancing in the Street
Martha & The Vandellas

40 Duke of Earl
Gene Chandler

42 Dust in the Wind
Kansas

48 Eleanor Rigby
The Beatles

51 Every Breath You Take
The Police

58 Fast Car
Tracy Chapman

70 Fire and Rain
James Taylor

65 Give Me One Reason
Tracy Chapman

74 Goodnight, Sweetheart, Goodnight
(Goodnight, It's Time to Go)
The Spaniels

76 Great Balls of Fire
Jerry Lee Lewis

79 The Great Pretender
The Platters

82 Heartbreak Hotel
Elvis Presley

90 Hey Jude
The Beatles

94 How Am I Supposed to
Live Without You
Michael Bolton

100 I Don't Want to Wait
Paula Cole

85 I Got You (I Feel Good)
James Brown

108 I Heard It Through the Grapevine
Marvin Gaye
Gladys Knight & The Pips

112 I'll Be There
Mariah Carey
The Jackson 5

120 If I Ever Lose My Faith in You
Sting

126 Imagine
John Lennon & The Plastic Ono

130 Invisible Touch
Genesis

134 It's Too Late
Carole King

117 Jailhouse Rock
Elvis Presley

138 Layla
Eric Clapton
Derek & The Dominos

143 Let It Be
The Beatles

148 Little Deuce Coupe
The Beach Boys

152 Maybe I'm Amazed
Paul McCartney

155 My Girl
The Temptations

162 Nights in White Satin
The Moody Blues

165 Oh, Pretty Woman
Roy Orbison

172 One More Night
Phil Collins

178 One Sweet Day
Mariah Carey and Boyz II Men

188 Operator (That's Not the Way It Feels)
Jim Croce

192 Our House
Crosy, Stills, Nash & Young

183 Penny Lane
The Beatles

200 Piano Man
Billy Joel

210 Sir Duke
Stevie Wonder

205 Something to Talk About (Let's Give Them Something to Talk About)
Bonnie Raitt

214 Spinning Wheel
Blood, Sweat & Tears

218 Start Me Up
The Rolling Stones

222 Stayin' Alive
The Bee Gees

227 Strawberry Fields Forever
The Beatles

230 Superstition
Stevie Wonder

234 Surf City
Jan & Dean

237 Surfin' U.S.A.
The Beach Boys

240 Sussudio
Phil Collins

251 Teach Your Children
Crosby, Stills, Nash & Young

258 Three Times a Lady
The Commodores

264 Time After Time
Cyndi Lauper
Inoj

268 Time in a Bottle
Jim Croce

272 Total Eclipse of the Heart
Bonnie Tyler

282 The Tracks of My Tears
The Miracles

286 Twist and Shout
The Beatles

279 Under the Boardwalk
The Drifters

290 A Whiter Shade of Pale
Procol Harum

293 Wild Thing
The Troggs

296 Will You Love Me Tomorrow
(Will You Still Love Me Tomorrow)
The Shirelles

300 You Can't Hurry Love
Phil Collins
The Supremes

ABC

Words and Music by ALPHONSO MIZELL, FREDERICK PERREN,
DEKE RICHARDS and BERRY GORDY

Bass Vamp

ANGEL

Words and Music by
SARAH McLACHLAN

Original key: D♭ major. This edition has been transposed down one half-step to be more playable.

ANOTHER DAY IN PARADISE

Words and Music by
PHIL COLLINS

To Coda ⊕

it

(%) Think a - bout __ it.

Oh Lord, __

is there no-thing more a - ny-bo-dy can do, __ oh __ Lord, __

there must be some-thing you __ can say. __

D.%. al Coda ⊕ **CODA**

It's just an - oth - er day___ for you and me,___ in pa - ra - dise.___ It's just an -

VERSE 2:

He walks on, doesn't look back,
He pretends he can't hear her,
Starts to whistle as he crosses the street,
Seems embarrased to be there.

VERSE 3:

She calls out to the man on the street,
He can see she's been crying,
She's got blisters on the soles of her feet,
She can't walk, but she's trying.

VERSE 4: (%)

You can tell from the lines on her face,
You can see that she's been there,
Probably been moved on from every place,
'Cos she didn't fit in there.

AT THE HOP

Words and Music by ARTHUR SINGER,
JOHN MADARA and DAVID WHITE

CRYING

Words and Music by ROY ORBISON
and JOE MELSON

BABY LOVE

Words and Music by BRIAN HOLLAND,
EDWARD HOLLAND and LAMONT DOZIER

BOHEMIAN RHAPSODY

Words and Music by
FREDDIE MERCURY

Slowly

Bb6   C7   Bb6 C7   F7   Cm7   F7

Is this the real life? Is this just fan-ta-sy? Caught in a land-slide, No es-

Bb   Cm7   Bb   Gm   Bb7

cape from re - al - i - ty. O - pen your eyes, __ Look up to the skies __ and

Eb   Cm   F7

see, I'm just a poor boy, I need no sym-pa-thy, Be-cause I'm

now I've gone and thrown it all a - way.
leave you all be - hind and face the truth.
Ma - ma __ ooh, ___

Ma - ma, __ ooh, ___

__ Did-n't mean to make you cry.
__ I don't want to die,
If I'm not back a - gain this time to -
I some-times wish I'd nev-er been born at

mor-row, car-ry on, car-ry on as if noth-ing real - ly mat - ters. __

DANCING IN THE STREET

Words and Music by MARVIN GAYE,
IVY HUNTER and WILLIAM STEVENSON

Moderately, with a steady beat

Call - ing out _ a - round _ the world, _ are you
in - vi - ta - tion a - cross the na - tion, a

read - y for a brand new beat? _ There'll be laugh - ing,
chance for folks to meet. _ Sum - mer's here _ and the
sing - ing _ and

time is right _ for danc - ing in the street. _ They're danc - ing in Chi -
mu - sic swing - ing, danc - ing in the street. _ Phil - a - del - phia, P. A.,

ca - go, ___ down in New Or - leans, __ Bal - ti - more and D. C., now.

in New York _ Cit - y. }
Can't for - get the Mo - tor _ Cit - y. }
All ___ we need __ is mu -

A

- sic, sweet _ mu - sic. There'll be mu - sic ev - 'ry - where. _

E7

__ There'll be swing-ing and sway - ing and re - cords play - ing,

DUKE OF EARL

Words and Music by EARL EDWARDS,
EUGENE DIXON and BERNICE WILLIAMS

Moderately with a rock beat

DUST IN THE WIND

Words and Music by
KERRY LIVGREN

Moderate Folk style

44

ev - 'ry - thing _ is dust in the wind.
wind.)

Repeat and Fade

Optional Ending

poco rit.

ELEANOR RIGBY

Words and Music by JOHN LENNON
and PAUL McCARTNEY

picks up the rice___ in the church___ where a wed - ding has been,___
writ - ing the words___ of a ser - mon that no___ one will hear,___
died in the church___ and was bur - ied a - long___ with her name,___

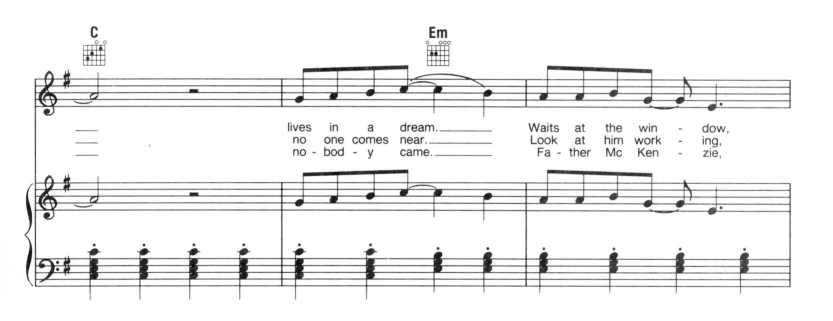

C   **Em**

___ lives in a dream._____ Waits at the win - dow,
___ no one comes near._____ Look at him work - ing,
___ no - bod - y came._____ Fa - ther Mc Ken - zie,

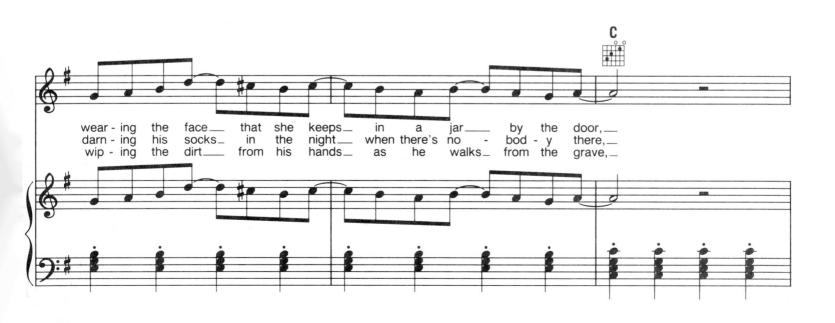

C

wear - ing the face___ that she keeps___ in a jar___ by the door,___
darn - ing his socks___ in the night___ when there's no - bod - y there,___
wip - ing the dirt___ from his hands___ as he walks___ from the grave,___

EVERY BREATH YOU TAKE

Written and Composed by
STING

Moderate Rock

long for your __ em-brace. I keep cry - ing, ba - by, ba - by, please__

FAST CAR

Words and Music by
TRACY CHAPMAN

You got a fast____ car.   I want a tic-ket   to an-y-where.
You got a fast____ car.   I got a plan   to get us out of here. I've been

May-be we make a deal.____   May-be to-geth-er we can get some-where.____
work-ing at the con-ve - nience store.   Man-aged to save____ just a lit-tle bit of mon-ey.

An - y place is bet-ter.____   Start-ing from ze-ro, got noth-ing to lose.
Won't have to drive too far,   just 'cross the bor-der and in - to the ci-ty.

GIVE ME ONE REASON

Words and Music by
TRACY CHAPMAN

Original key: F♯ major. This edition has been transposed up one half-step to be more playable.

FIRE AND RAIN

Words and Music by
JAMES TAYLOR

Verse 3:

GOODNIGHT, SWEETHEART, GOODNIGHT

(Goodnight, It's Time to Go)

Words and Music by JAMES HUDSON
and CALVIN CARTER

GREAT BALLS OF FIRE

Words and Music by OTIS BLACKWELL
and JACK HAMMER

THE GREAT PRETENDER

Words and Music by
BUCK RAM

HEARTBREAK HOTEL

Words and Music by MAE BOREN AXTON,
TOMMY DURDEN and ELVIS PRESLEY

I GOT YOU
(I Feel Good)

Words and Music by
JAMES BROWN

HEY JUDE

Words and Music by JOHN LENNON
and PAUL McCARTNEY

HOW AM I SUPPOSED TO LIVE WITHOUT YOU

Words and Music by MICHAEL BOLTON
and DOUG JAMES

I could hard-ly be-lieve___ it, when I
I'm too proud for cry-___ing, did-n't

heard the news___ to-day.___ I had to come___ and get it straight___ from you.
come here to break down.___ It's just a dream of mine___ is com-in' to___ an end.___

They said you are leav-___ in' some-one's
And how can I blame___ you when I

98

I DON'T WANT TO WAIT

Words and Music by
PAULA COLE

I HEARD IT
THROUGH THE GRAPEVINE

Words and Music by NORMAN J. WHITFIELD
and BARRETT STRONG

D.S. al Coda

Peo - ple say be - lieve half __

CODA

__ yeah, yeah, __ yeah. I heard it through the grape-vine, not much

Repeat and Fade

lon - ger would you be mine, ba - by. Yeah, __

I'LL BE THERE

Words and Music by BERRY GORDY, HAL DAVIS,
WILLIE HUTCH and BOB WEST

JAILHOUSE ROCK

Words and Music by JERRY LEIBER
and MIKE STOLLER

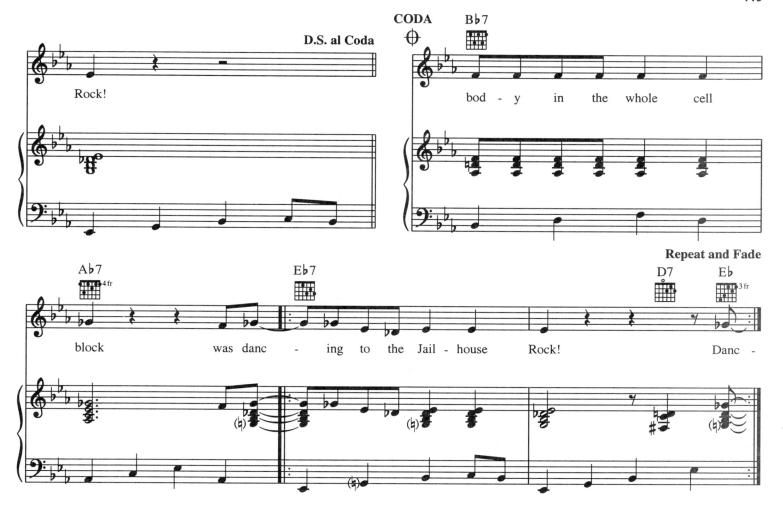

Additional Lyrics

2. Spider Murphy played the tenor saxophone
Little Joe was blowin' on the slide trombone.
The drummer boy from Illinois went crash, boon, bang;
The whole rhythm section was the Purple Gang.
(Chorus)

3. Number Forty-seven said to number Three:
"You're the cutest jailbird I ever did see.
I sure would be delighted with your company,
Come on and do the Jailhouse Rock with me."
(Chorus)

4. The sad sack was a-sittin' on a block of stone,
Way over in the corner weeping all alone.
The warden said: "Hey, Buddy, don't you be no square,
If you can't find a partner, use a wooden chair!"
(Chorus)

5. Shifty Henry said to Bugs: "For heaven's sake,
No one's lookin', now's our chance to make a break."
Bugsy turned to Shifty and he said: "Nix, nix;
I wanna stick around a while and get my kicks."
(Chorus)

IF I EVER LOSE MY FAITH IN YOU

Written and Composed by
STING

You could say   I   lost ___ my   faith   in ___ sci -
Some would say   I   was ___ a   lost ___ man   in   a ___ lost
I   nev - er   saw   no   mir - a - cle   of   sci - ence

ence   and   prog - ress.
world.

IMAGINE

Words and Music by
JOHN LENNON

INVISIBLE TOUCH

Words and Music by TONY BANKS,
PHIL COLLINS and MIKE RUTHERFORD

IT'S TOO LATE

Words by TONI STERN
Music by CAROLE KING

LAYLA

Words and Music by ERIC CLAPTON
and JIM GORDON

Original key: Eb minor. This edition has been transposed up one whole-step to be more playable.

LET IT BE

Words and Music by JOHN LENNON
and PAUL McCARTNEY

When I find my-self ___ in times of trou-ble,
Instrumental

Moth-er Mar - y comes to me speak-ing words of wis - dom; let it

be. ___ And in my hour of dark - ness, she is

LITTLE DEUCE COUPE

Music by BRIAN WILSON
Words by ROGER CHRISTIAN

four on the floor— yeah, she purrs like a kit- ten till the lake pipes roar, — and

if that ain't e - nough to make you flip your wig, — there's one more thing, I've got the

pink slip, dad - dy! And com - in' off the line, when the lights turn green, — she

MAYBE I'M AMAZED

Words and Music by
PAUL McCARTNEY

MY GIRL

Words and Music by WILLIAM "SMOKEY" ROBINSON
and RONALD WHITE

NIGHTS IN WHITE SATIN

Words and Music by
JUSTIN HAYWARD

OH, PRETTY WOMAN

Words and Music by ROY ORBISON
and BILL DEES

night.

Pret-ty wom-an ____ don't walk on by, ____ Pret-ty wom-an ____ don't make me cry, ____ Pret-ty wom-an ____ don't walk a-way. ____

170

ONE MORE NIGHT

Words and Music by
PHIL COLLINS

One more night,___

one more night.___

I've been try-ing for___ so long ___ to
I've been sit-ting here___ so long ___
I know there'll nev-er be___ a time ___ you'll ev-er

174

175

ONE SWEET DAY

Words and Music by MARIAH CAREY, WALTER AFANASIEFF,
SHAWN STOCKMAN, MICHAEL McCARY,
NATHAN MORRIS and WANYA MORRIS

PENNY LANE

Words and Music by JOHN LENNON
and PAUL McCARTNEY

OPERATOR
(That's Not the Way It Feels)

Words and Music by
JIM CROCE

OUR HOUSE

Words and Music by
GRAHAM NASH

PIANO MAN

Words and Music by
BILLY JOEL

Page 204

SOMETHING TO TALK ABOUT
(Let's Give Them Something to Talk About)

Words and Music by
SHIRLEY EIKHARD

Moderate Reggae/Rock

People are talk-ing, talk-ing a-bout peo-ple.
I feel so fool-ish. I nev-er no-ticed that,

I hear them whis-per, you won't be-lieve it.
ba-by, you're act-ing so nerv-ous, like you're fall-ing.

* Recorded a half step lower

Let's   give them some-thing to talk a-bout.
Come on, give them some-thing to talk a-bout,

Let's give them_ some-thing to
a   lit-tle_ mys-t'ry to

talk a-bout._
fig-ure out._

I wan-na give them some-thing to talk   a-bout.   I want your love._

And —

SIR DUKE

Words and Music by
STEVIE WONDER

Mu-sic is a world with-in it-self _____ with a
Mu-sic knows it is and al-ways will _____ be one of

lan-guage we all un-der-stand, ____
the things that life just won't quit. ____

SPINNING WHEEL

Words and Music by
DAVID CLAYTON THOMAS

START ME UP

Words and Music by MICK JAGGER
and KEITH RICHARDS

219

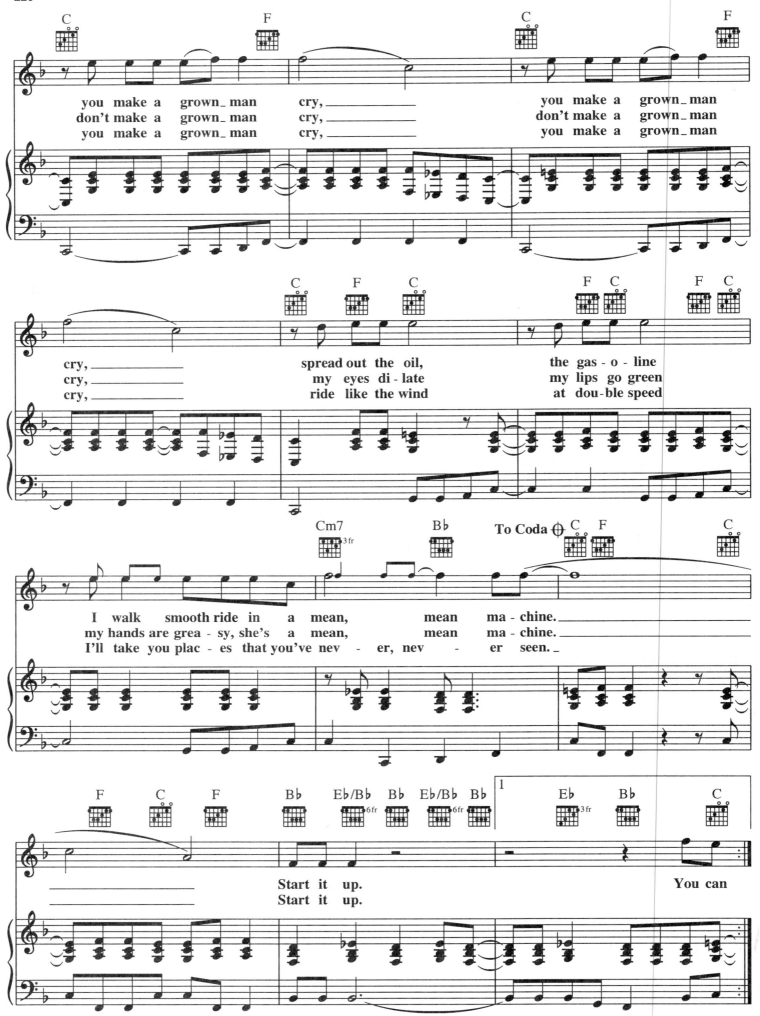

STAYIN' ALIVE

Words and Music by BARRY GIBB,
MAURICE GIBB and ROBIN GIBB

224

STRAWBERRY FIELDS FOREVER

Words and Music by JOHN LENNON
and PAUL McCARTNEY

SUPERSTITION

Words and Music by
STEVIE WONDER

Moderate Funk

E♭m

mf

1

2

Ver - y su - per - sti -

(Segno)

- tious, ___
- tious. ___
- tious. ___

writ-ings on the wall. ___
Wash your face and hands. ___
Noth-ing more to say. ____

Ver - y su - per - sti - tious, ___
Rid me of the prob - lems. ___
Ver - y su - per - sti - tious. ___

lad-der's 'bout ___ to fall. ___
Do all that ___ you can. ___
The dev - il's on ___ his way. ___

SURF CITY

Words and Music by BRIAN WILSON
and JAN BERRY

SURFIN' U.S.A.

Words and Music by
CHUCK BERRY

Solid shuffle beat

If ev-'ry-bod-y had an o-cean a-cross the U. S. A.
(We'll all be plan-nin' out a) route we're gon-na take real soon

Then ev-'ry-bod-y'd be surf - in'
We're wax-in' down our surf boards

like Cal-i-for-ni-a. You'd see them wear-in' their
we can't wait for June. We'll all be gone for the

SUSSUDIO

Words and Music by
PHIL COLLINS

Moderate dance beat

There's a

TEACH YOUR CHILDREN

Words and Music by
GRAHAM NASH

You ... who are on the road ____

world before that they we can can live die. in.)

D.S. al Coda

CODA

love you.

THREE TIMES A LADY

Words and Music by
LIONEL RICHIE

TIME AFTER TIME

Words and Music by CYNDI LAUPER
and ROB HYMAN

TIME IN A BOTTLE

Words and Music by
JIM CROCE

TOTAL ECLIPSE OF THE HEART

Words and Music by
JIM STEINMAN

night
Once u- pon a time I was fal- ling in love But now I'm on- ly fal- ling a- part.

There's no- thing I can do A tot- al e- clipse__ of the heart__

Once up- on a time there was light in my life, but now there's on- ly love in the dark.

Verse 3:

Turn around
Every now and then I know you'll never be the boy you always wanted to be
Turn around.
But every now and then I know you'll always be the only boy who wanted me the way that I am
Turn around.
Every now and then I know there's no-one in the universe as magical and wonderous as you
Turn around.
Every now and then I know there's nothing any better there's nothing that I just wouldn't do

Chorus:

Turn around bright eyes
Every now and then I fall apart
Turn around bright eyes
Every now and then I fall apart

Middle:

And I need you now tonight, and I need you more than ever
And if you'll only hold me tight we'll be holding on forever
And we'll only be making it right cause we'll never be wrong together
We can take it to the end of the line.
Your love is like a shadow on me all the time
I don't know what to do and I'm always in the dark
We're living in a powder keg and giving off sparks

I really need you tonight, forever's gonna start tonight, forever's gonna start tonight

Once upon a time I was falling in love, but now I'm only falling apart
Nothing I can do, a total eclipse of the heart
Once upon a time there was light in my life, but now there's only love in the dark
Nothing I can say, a total eclipse of the heart
A total eclipse of the heart

Turn around bright eyes
Turn around bright eyes
Turn around.

UNDER THE BOARDWALK

Words and Music by ARTIE RESNICK
and KENNY YOUNG

THE TRACKS OF MY TEARS

Words and Music by WILLIAM "SMOKEY" ROBINSON,
WARREN MOORE and MARVIN TARPLIN

Do, do, do, ___ doot. Do, do, do, ___ doot. Do, do, do, ___ doot. Do, do, do, do, do, do. ___

Peo - ple say I'm the
Since you left me, if you

life of the par - ty 'cause ___ I tell a joke or two. ___ Al - though I
see me with an - oth - er girl, seem - in' like I'm hav - in' fun. ___ Al - though she

TWIST AND SHOUT

Words and Music by BERT RUSSELL
and PHIL MEDLEY

A WHITER SHADE OF PALE

Words and Music by KEITH REID
and GARY BROOKER

WILD THING

Words and Music by
CHIP TAYLOR

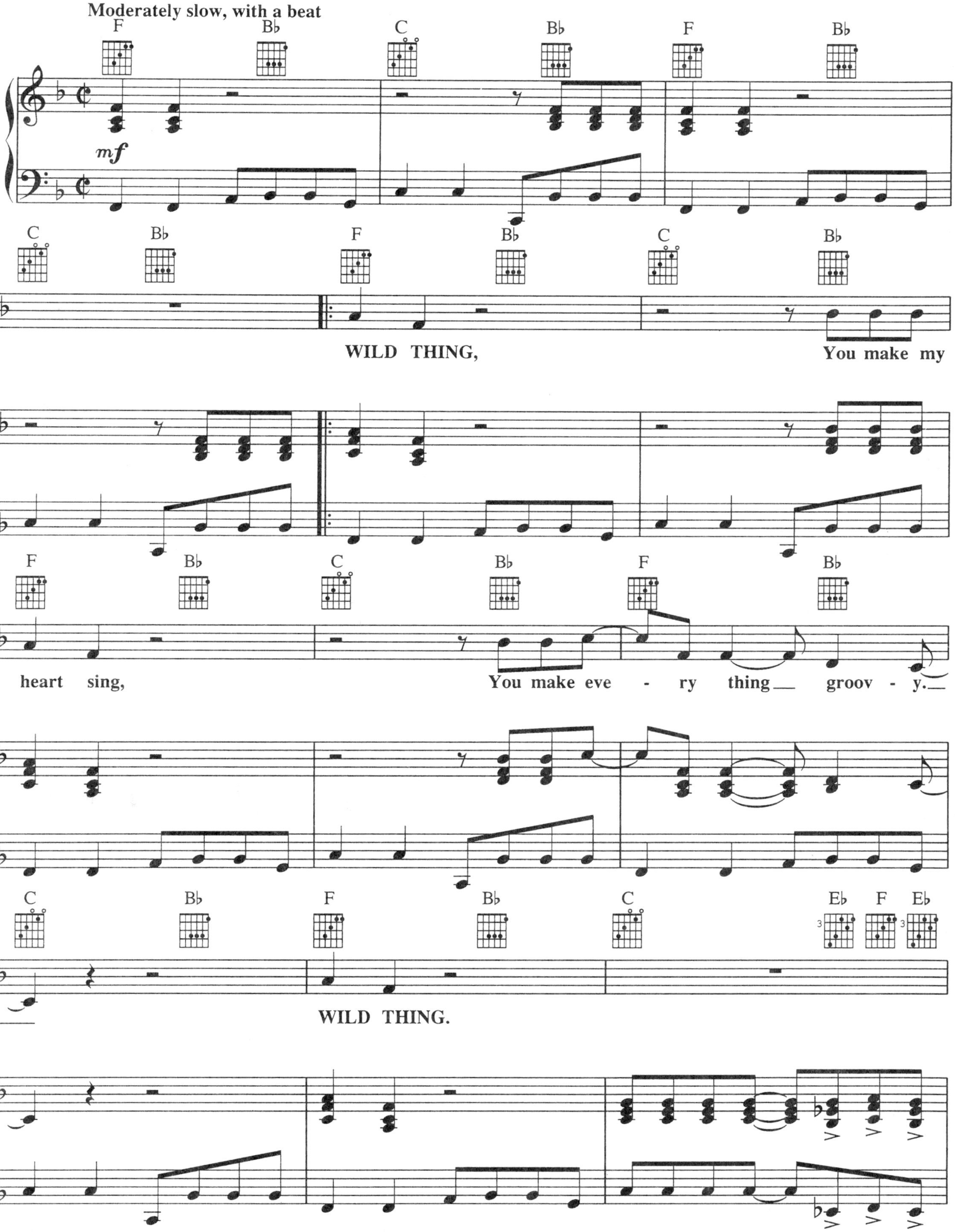
Moderately slow, with a beat
F Bb C Bb F Bb
mf
C Bb F Bb C Bb
WILD THING, You make my
F Bb C Bb F Bb
heart sing, You make eve - ry thing groov - y.
C Bb F Bb C Eb F Eb
WILD THING.

WILD THING, I ___ think I love you. But I wan - na know
WILD THING, I ___ think you move me. But I wan - na know

___ for sure.
___ for sure.

Come on and hold me tight. ___
Come on and hold me tight. ___

I love you.
You move me.

WILL YOU LOVE ME TOMORROW
(Will You Still Love Me Tomorrow)

Words and Music by GERRY GOFFIN
and CAROLE KING

YOU CAN'T HURRY LOVE

Words and Music by EDWARD HOLLAND,
LAMONT DOZIER and BRIAN HOLLAND